SUPERNATURAL

A Study Guide

SUPERNATURAL

A Study Guide

Ronn Johnson

LEXHAM PRESS

Supernatural: A Study Guide

Copyright 2016 Ronn Johnson

Lexham Press, 1313 Commercial St., Bellingham, WA 98225
LexhamPress.com

Unless otherwise noted, Scripture quotations are the author's
translation.

Print ISBN 9781577996842
Digital ISBN 9781577996859

Lexham Editorial Team: Lynnea Fraser
Typesetting: ProjectLuz.com

To Susan

CONTENTS

ACKNOWLEDGMENTS

My friendship with Mike Heiser goes back many years, and I wish to thank him for the opportunity to write this study guide as an accompaniment to *Supernatural*. I also want to thank the common friends that we share in this project, as well as my students over the years who have heard me teach on the subject of gods and angels. We all acknowledge this subject remains a work in progress. I mostly wish to thank my wife, Susan, who has faithfully been by my side for 29 years and who continues to be my biggest fan, most inspiring coach, and finest critic.

Until a dozen years ago I read the Bible assuming that "gods" (note the small *g*) were imaginary beings, something invented by the human mind. I took the first commandment ("You shall have no other gods before me") to mean that God did not want me to love boats or cars or money more than himself. This way of reading the Bible made sense to me, and it worked just fine as I made my way through Bible college and seminary. Small *g* "gods" did not exist, and I had no reason to think differently since I was surrounded by people who believed the same.

One day (we're still a dozen years ago) I had breakfast with a visiting friend at a local coffee shop. We had gone to school together and were both now in the dissertation stages of our PhD programs. I was not that interested in what I was writing about, to be honest, so I was curious to hear about his subject. I could sense that he was fascinated by what he was researching. He began drawing on napkins, doodling his way through an explanation of ancient Near Eastern and biblical texts. After a few minutes I was compelled to interrupt him with an urgent question: "So wait a second—are you saying that Moses believed the gods of the first commandment *were actually real?*"

"No," he said dryly. "I'm saying he would have been surprised by the question."

This friend, as it turns out, is the author of *Supernatural*. Since that day in the coffee shop, Mike Heiser has become the leading evangelical writer, blogger, and researcher in the subject of the gods of the Bible. Those who have followed his work have realized that his goal is simple, yet challenging: *He wants people who believe the Bible to understand the Bible they say they believe.* Many evangelicals write with this goal in mind, but no one has done so while defending the reality of the gods of the first commandment. In tracking with Mike's argument you will be introduced, likely for the first time, to a view of the Bible that takes these gods seriously. And I agree with Mike—I think Moses would be surprised that it took this long for such a book to be written.

This study guide is intended to work alongside the book *Supernatural*, offering material for review and thoughts for further study and application. Each chapter in the guide corresponds to two chapters of the book. *Supernatural* will set the course for your study about the gods, doing most of the heavy lifting along the way, with this guide trailing behind, considering where one idea affects another. It is my sincere hope that you never read the Bible the same way again. Welcome to the world of *Supernatural*.

—Ronn Johnson

ONE SMALL CHANGE, ONE BIG DIFFERENCE

Read Supernatural, *chapters 1–2. Read and prepare to discuss*
1 Kings 22:19–23; Psalm 82; Daniel 4:13–27; 7:9–10.

The Big Picture

Surveys taken within the past decade show that three-fourths of Americans believe in the supernatural world of God and angels. Christians heartily embrace the concept of the supernatural, presuming that the Bible's description of spirits, demons, and miracles must be true in order for Scripture to have any consistent meaning.

However, we do face a challenge. Our modern, Western Christian culture seems content with an approach to the Bible which tends to tame or quiet its supernatural element. Think of the story of Noah and the ark, with its pairs of animals streaming to the boat. Every child can picture this. But it's not so easy to recall the odd event which led up to it. Preachers are tempted to skip over the sons of God marrying the daughters of men (Gen 6:1–4) — whatever that means — hoping to get to the more sensible story of the flood. As a result, what the writer wanted to accomplish may be lost because we're uncomfortable with what appears to be a *super*-natural moment in the story. We can only imagine how this harms the meaning of the Bible on a larger scale.

Supernatural and this study guide will challenge your thinking concerning the supernatural world of the Bible. At the heart of this challenge is a simple question, which sets in motion all that is to follow: Are the "gods" of the first commandment ("You shall have no other gods before me") real, personal beings? For whatever reason, most readers of the Bible have not given this question serious consideration. You may have never thought it to be a question at all. Regardless, consider this book as your unique opportunity to experience the Bible with the view that gods actively live in the heavens and function as gods do. This challenge will be as fascinating as it is enjoyable, and it will result in a deep appreciation for the full story of Scripture.

A quick illustration may help get us going. Imagine a wife overhearing her husband talking on the phone. She first gets suspicious, then jealous, as she hears him share intimate conversation. Finally, she has had enough and grabs the phone to confront the caller. To her surprise, no one is there. He had been speaking to a dial tone.

In this light, consider what God meant in Deuteronomy 6:14–15: "You shall not go after other gods, the gods of the peoples who are all around you—for the LORD your God is a jealous God—lest the anger of the LORD your God be aroused against you and destroy you from the face of the earth" (NKJV adapted). Would the Israelites have been tempted to worship what only amounted to a dial tone? Or would they have faced temptation to worship real gods in Canaan?

The Main Idea

The challenge in accepting the reality of "gods" begins by demystifying the concept. We must immediately appeal to Hebrew and Greek, the original languages of the Bible. English simply will not do. Let's review what we read in the opening chapter of *Supernatural*: The most common word in the Old Testament for "God" is *elohim*, appearing about 6,200 times. We come upon this word immediately in Genesis 1:1: "In the beginning *elohim* created the heavens and the earth." The Bible opens with a clear and certain claim that one *elohim* created the entire universe. But more work remains to be done.

Who or what is an *elohim*? It's actually a broad title (not a name) which can be translated as "God," "god," "godhead," "spirit," "deity," "divine being," or "strong one"—with each option carrying its own theological agenda. Variants of this word appear in languages throughout the ancient Near East, suggesting that *elohim* and its meaning was borrowed from secular societies which predated Israel and Moses. Other nations talked about their *elohim* all the time, often in very loving and appreciative tones. Like our word "Dad," which we use as a title for the man we know and honor, people in the Bible and other pagan cultures speak about "their *elohim*" or "the *elohim* of my fathers/land" with regularity.

So how do you know where the word *elohim* appears in an English Bible? Generally, you can follow this rule: Wherever you see the word "God" or "god" or "gods" in your Old Testament, you can be confident that the original reads *elohim*. Easy enough. The challenge begins in trying to decide whether "God" or "god" or "gods" should be used when translating *elohim*. More details will follow later. For now, just remember that when we speak of "God" or "gods" in the Old Testament, we're actually talking about the single Hebrew word *elohim*. (In the New Testament, the Greek word for "God" or "god" is *theos*.)

Does this prove that the gods of the first commandment are real? No, we have more work to do. But the very fact that "God" and "god" are the same word in Hebrew or Greek should lead us to presume in the reality of each *elohim/theos* until we discover evidence otherwise.

Digging Deeper

Jesus encouraged us to pray, "May your will be done on earth *as it is done in heaven*." This sounds as if God's will is already being accomplished in a heavenly or spiritual world before being accomplished in our own. Could it be that Jesus knew that a society of spirits existed above us, actively engaged in doing God's will? It certainly seems so, and it is just this kind of text that we will be looking at throughout our study—texts which give us reason to appreciate the reality of the spirit world and the society they likely enjoy. As you read the references included in this guide, notice that some of the quietest narratives in the Bible depend on spirits functioning as a society among themselves before affecting human beings on earth.

It would be helpful to confront a common question before we get further into our study: What is an *angel*, especially in relation to a *god*? Most people believe these words refer to very different things, causing them to say, "I can believe in angels, but not in gods." It is here that a large-scale change needs to be made with regard to how we think of angels.

For example, Psalm 97:7 says, "Worship him, all you *elohim*," demanding that the gods worship their creator, the God of Israel. When the New Testament quotes this verse in Hebrews 1:6, the writer says it this way: "Let all the angels [Greek, *angeloi*] of God worship him." Where *elohim*, or "gods," appear in Psalm 97, "angels" appear in Hebrews 1. Very simply, we will find that *angels are gods*, and that gods can sometimes function as angels. Again, more on this later.

Knowledge in Action

Henry Ford was famous for his automobile assembly line, but behind the scenes he depended heavily on the mechanical engineering skills of his friend Charles Stein-metz. On one occasion, Ford's assembly line ground to a halt for reasons no one could understand. In a panic, Ford asked Steinmetz to see if he could make the necessary repairs.

Steinmetz was happy to help his friend, and it wasn't long before the assembly line was up and running. Ford was pleased, of course, until he looked at the bill—Stein-metz wanted $10,000.

"Charles, you can't be serious," Ford complained. "You tinkered in there for about ten minutes."

"You're right," Steinmetz admitted, "I made a mistake." He took the bill and changed it to *Tinkering: $10. Knowing where to tinker: $9,990.*

This story reminds us of the challenge in understanding the Bible. We make an adjustment here, an interpretive move there. Sometimes the changes we make are large, but more often they're small. As we make adjustments to our interpretations, we try to keep track of how the Bible reads differently, and hopefully more clearly, when applying one change and possibly dispensing with another. It's like test-driving a car. We read the Bible hoping that someday, with time and care in the process of making trial runs with its multiple dead ends and periodic successes, we will experience a smooth running story of Scripture that hugs every curve and climbs every hill with ease.

Think about the challenge that awaits you. This study and *Supernatural* propose what is actually a very small change—a small tinkering with the text, if you will—but one which will likely have far-reaching results: *Do other gods exist? And what would the Bible sound like if they did?*

Discussion Questions

- To date, what effort have you given to considering the question, "Are the gods of the first commandment real?" What are the reasons behind your answer?

  _____

  _____

  _____

- The story of 1 Kings 22 was discussed in chapter 1 of *Supernatural*. Did you read this story before? If so, how did you interpret what was going on?

  _____

  _____

  _____

- We will be discussing the concept of idols in coming sections of our study. But what are your initial
  thoughts about them? Why do you think idols have
  played such a major role in religion, and how are
  they related to the concept of a god?

  _____

  _____

  _____

- On the front end—before getting into the meat of
  our study—what do you predict will change in your
  interpretation of the Bible if small-*g* gods do exist?

  _____

  _____

  _____

CHAPTER 2

REBELLION OF THE GODS

Read Supernatural, *chapters 3–4. Read and prepare to discuss*
Genesis 1–3; 6:1–8.

The Big Picture

In chapters 3–4 of *Supernatural*, we learned about God's
original home, the garden of Eden. The garden was a
place of God's physical presence, a locatable spot on the
earth where the Creator could meet with humankind and
commune with them in perfect fellowship. When Adam
and Eve disobeyed and were kicked out of the garden,
our attention is drawn to both what they lost and what
they gained.

What they had lost, of course, was the immediate fa-
vor of God. Several curses were to follow them through
life. But what they had gained is important as well, as noted at the conclusion of the story: "Then the LORD God said,
'Behold, the man has become like one of Us, to know good

and evil' " (Gen 3:22 NKJV). Adam's sin led him to be awakened to knowledge that he had not had before. Adam now had the "knowledge of good and evil," and God was not pleased. It was time for Adam and Eve to leave the garden and to have the door bolted behind them. Estrangement from God came along with estrangement from his garden. But with this estrangement also came a kind of knowledge that would come to haunt humankind. More on this as we go.

Biblical writers often return to the memory of Eden at other critical moments. For example, during the exodus from Egypt, Israel was led to the place where God would eventually "put his name" (Deut 12:5). God intended to re-establish a physical place to identify as his own, and this would have reminded the Israelites of what Adam had earlier enjoyed. In his prophecy, Ezekiel mentions Eden by name when speaking of the future hope of a restored and faithful Israel (Ezek 36:35). This introduces us to the concept described in *Supernatural* as "cosmic geography." Land, borders, hills, rivers, and even physical clods of dirt carried spiritual meaning, notably because spiritual forces were assumed to exercise territorial ownership. Eden is just the beginning. Hang on to this critical idea as we continue in our study.

The Main Idea

"Houston, we have a problem." At some point in the story— we are never explicitly told when or how or why—evil spirits came into existence. There are many unanswered questions regarding the origin of evils spirits, or the gods of the first commandment. Tradition and poetry (such as Dante's *Inferno*) have tended to confuse us, giving us more information than the Bible. All we know for sure, in returning to our story, is that as Adam and Eve left the garden they were venturing into a world under dominion of the divine rebel of Eden, who had been "cast down" to earth, and where rival gods would emerge who were hostile to the people loyal to the true God. Above them the sign flashed, "Mankind, you have a problem."

This problem, we learn all too quickly, is that heavenly disloyalty among spirits is about to spread to the humans who worship them. To sins of all varieties, mankind will add the act of flagrant rebellion—the kind of rebellion where a man is caught saying intimate things to the person on the other end of the phone. God's jealousy will burn, like a scorned wife who is left alone at her door. Hosea uses a close illustration: "When Israel was a child, I loved him, and out of Egypt I called My son. ... [Yet] they sacrificed to the Baals, and burned incense to carved images" (Hosea 11:1-2 NKJV).

We can now see the urgency of the first commandment. "You shall have no other *elohim* before me" was not talking about giving attention to money or boats or cars. It was God's jealous love on full display, pointing directly to the most dangerous element of his creation—the world of supernatural creatures who, for some reason, enjoy human worship—while also eerily predicting what would happen before the coming of Christ. "You shall make no covenant with [the Canaanites], nor with their gods. They shall not dwell in your land, lest they make you sin against Me. For if you serve their gods, it will surely be a snare to you" (Exod 23:32–33 NKJV). "You have uncovered yourself to those other than [God]," Isaiah later tells the Israelites. "You have gone up to them, and have enlarged your bed and have made a covenant with them. You have loved their bed" (Isa 57:8 NKJV adapted). The Great Commandment was broken.

Digging Deeper

It's interesting that Old Testament writers take little interest in Adam and Eve. Their story is not mentioned again after Genesis 3. What is not lost on later writers, however, is Adam's willingness to listen and obey a spirit who was not his Creator. He sinned in disobeying a command about a tree and fruit, but even more so he sinned in obeying the wrong voice. He disobeyed one *elohim* to obey another, and this will form the larger story of the Old Testament: "Go and cry out to the gods which you have chosen; let them deliver you in your time of distress" (Judg 10:14 NKJV). No wonder Adam hid from God. He was afraid that his disloyalty would be discovered.

In this light, consider how the "sons of God" appear in Genesis 6 as though they are expected players on the stage. As we read in *Supernatural*, the title "sons of" can have the simple meaning of "those to be identified as" (much

like "sons of men" can simply mean "human," 2 Sam 7:14).
When played off the "daughters of men" in Genesis 6:4,
the clear meaning of the story is that *elohim* interrupt-
ed themselves into human affairs. Yes, it sounds odd. But
as I like to remind myself, I cannot get into the habit of
taking all the odd verses out of the Bible. We believe in
a truly supernatural world, created by God to include a
society of men and spirits who have immediate contact
with each other on various levels and in mysterious ways.
In short, the Bible presumes a world in which God and
gods regularly involve themselves with humans. As one
of my teachers liked to say as he turned to the next page
in his notes ... *get used to it*.

Knowledge in Action

As *Supernatural* explains, the image of God is best understood as a role we play in God's creation. It is our stewardship to rule our planet and to rule it well. This idea
of stewardship is sometimes detectible in how the Bible
speaks of "glory." We glorify someone when we speak well
of them (compare Acts 13:48). When used as a noun, "glory" can refer to "doing well with" what one owns or has
been given (Prov 25:2; Jer 21:5; Isa 46:13, "Israel my glory").
So we can think of our "image" as a gift from God, a stewardship of rule, which we have unfortunately lost because
of our disloyalty to our Creator (Rom 3:23, "fallen short of
the glory of God"). Humankind has handed the privilege
of rule over to the beings they have chosen to worship.

When people are full of care about something, we can call them "careful." A situation is "stressful" when it is full of stress. So it is in the Bible when dealing with the words "faith" and "faithful." When a person has faith, and has a lot of it, he or she is said to be faithful. Our English language often distinguishes faith from faithfulness—the first having to do with what we believe, and the second with how we act—and this is desperately unfortunate. "Faith" and "faithful" arise from the same Hebrew and Greek words. The importance of this understanding relates to the meaning of faith, and why the story of salvation in both Testaments revolves around becoming faithful to the right God. The issue, as we will see, is one of loyalty. The sin of idolatry will not be like just any other sin. It will be *the sin*, the operative indiscretion of sending our loyalty to another person or being who is not our Creator. This is why salvation in the Bible is always described in *faith*-ing terms. God is not ultimately looking for better behavior. He is looking for faith, or loyalty.

You may have heard of the term "spiritual warfare." While it appears that this idea can be overused, there is a sense in which we need to speak about it now, just after Adam and Eve leave the garden. Adam is heading into a real war, where temptation to honor and serve and love other gods will be the basic temptation of humankind (Jer 8:2). Wars between nations will be thought of in terms of disputes to be settled between gods (Judg 11:23-24), and Joshua's battles leave no doubt as to God's ultimate control of the enemy (Josh 11:19-20). As a practical matter, Paul will later call the kind of sufferings that relate to our spiritual war as "sufferings of the gospel" (2 Tim 1:8). We will certainly return to the concept of spiritual warfare in later discussion.

Discussion Questions

- Why do you think God said, "Let us make man in our image," instead of the more expected "I will make man in my image"? What are the implications that come out of this choice of words?

  _____

  _____

  _____

- Should we fault the original writers and readers of the Bible for thinking that God actually "lived" or existed on a particular plot of ground? Read 2 Chronicles 30:27 and try to discern Solomon's understanding of where God actually "exists." What difference does this make to our story?

  _____

  _____

  _____

- How are faith and faithfulness related in your understanding of what it means to be (or become) a Christian?

  _____

  _____

  _____

- An unhealthy understanding of spiritual warfare can be dangerous. Why is this the case?

  _____

  _____

  _____

CHAPTER 3

COSMIC GEOGRAPHY

Read Supernatural, *chapters 5–6. Read and prepare to discuss Genesis 11:1–9; 12:1–7; 15:1–6; Deuteronomy 32:1–9.*

The Big Picture

The scene in Genesis 11 is of Babel, with the people of the world gathered to worship from the top of a tall structure. When God said, "Let us go down and confuse their language" (11:7), we are reminded of what he had said as Adam and Eve left the garden of Eden: "Now they have become like one of us" (3:22). The "us" in each case suggests that God was bringing the situation to the attention of someone else. And in both cases God sends the offending people *out*, or *away* from where they had been living. These scenes introduce the idea of cosmic geography, where God used land—physically defined borders, inherited rights of ownership, even the dirt in its fields— to tell the story of his people and their ultimate salvation. *Supernatural* carefully describes the critical moment after the Tower of Babel incident in which God apportioned or divided the world to the interests and powers of created spirits. This theme of spirit-controlled land influences a surprising number of Old Testament narratives and conversations, coming to full bloom in the ministry of Jesus Christ. It is critical to appreciate this in light of upcoming chapters.

The God who valued physical land also valued the physical human body. Ancient civilizations presumed that gods or spirits did not normally inhabit the flesh of humans ("the gods, whose dwelling is not with flesh"; Dan 2:11 NKJV). Yet we read of numerous examples of God appearing in human form, often for the purpose of explaining his will to someone facing a critical decision. It was God's way of taking personal interest in people who so often needed a personal touch. We still need this today. I recently heard a man say, "I struggle with the concept of God ... but I do believe that Jesus lived, died, and rose again to be the Lord of the world. I can understand and believe that." He was describing how cosmic geography works. God has, through Christ, come to re-own that which he already owned: this physical home we call Earth.

The Main Idea

The sooner we understand the largest story in the Bible, the sooner we can appreciate its smaller sub-stories and individual plot lines. There is, of course, some debate in trying to identify the largest story of the Bible. Is it Adam and Eve, and the deeds of their offspring? Or is it their sin, their eating of the fruit, that led to the pain and death which we now experience daily? Many would say the Bible is about Jesus, and our privilege of going to heaven if we believe in him. While all of these are important themes in the Bible, I believe that the principal story of Scripture is *Abraham's loyalty to God while refusing to worship the spiritual forces which sought his destruction*. The story of Abraham eventually finds fulfillment in the Messiah. All the smaller parts of the story will find their proper expression through Abraham, his family, and their relationships to God and the gods.

How does this relate to our study about the spiritual world? Recall where the story of Abraham is placed: immediately after the worldwide flood and the subsequent apportionment of lands and peoples to the authority of created gods (Deut 4:19; 29:26; 32:8). The Psalmist recalls these combined incidents as when God "sat enthroned at the flood" (Psa 29:10), delegating his leadership over creation by commanding the stewardship of gods within it. When Abraham is called by God to turn away from his worship of the god of the city of Ur (Josh 24:2; Gen 12:1–3) we are drawn into a story with fascinating possibilities: What will it mean to follow one *elohim* over another? What is Abraham's *elohim* like? Will this man get any land out of the deal—especially when leaving his home behind? Will his family continue his legacy of worshiping this *elohim*? Or, more important, will Abraham's *elohim* reward him and his family for their loyalty, and if so, how?

Digging Deeper

We have the privilege of knowing how Abraham's story goes. His family, the nation of Israel, will make the mistake of thinking that their God would not abandon them or their land even if they started to worship the gods of other nations. They were wrong. They exchanged God's "good laws," meant for their physical and moral benefit (Deut 5:15), for the ways of gods who hated the very humans who worshiped them (Jer 7:31; 1 Pet 1:18). On account of their disloyalty, Israel was sent to suffer in exile, forced to live under the authority of the gods now recognized as liars (Ezek 21:29) who "could not save" after all (Isa 45:20). The country of Israel now sat quiet and abandoned. The land and its people went fallow, awaiting the day when God would restore their fortunes and faithfulness.

The fact that Jesus may have appeared in the Old Testament adds depth to this larger story. Israel had been taught by precept and experience that God would save his people through designated human intervention. Remember that God values the personal touch! Whether through a judge, a king, or an anonymous woman dropping a millstone from a window (Judg 9:53), Israel had consistent reason to believe that God would physically come to its rescue. He did many times. God's ultimate promise of salvation, however, was always connected with Israel's restored fidelity. "Afterward the children of Israel shall return, seek the Lord their God and David their king, and fear the Lord and his goodness in the latter days"

(Hos 3:5 NKJV adapted). We notice that David, long dead, was the hope of Israel *along with God*. We will study at a later point this concept of *binitarianism*, or the honoring of God alongside his appointed Messiah.

Knowledge in Action

You have probably heard that idolatry comes in all sorts of colors, including the love of things, pride, or that promotion at work. In this sense the second commandment ("You shall not make a graven image") has been interpreted in light of the tenth ("You shall not covet"). But is this what idolatry meant to the original writers and readers of the Bible? Not at all. In each of its biblical occurrences, the sin of idolatry describes the worship of a real deity through the use of a physical manipulative made of stone, metal, or wood. It led to what Paul called "fellowshiping with demons" (1 Cor 10:20), recalling the singular sin that led Israel into exile. It would likely come as a complete surprise to Moses or Paul that a car (or a camel) could be considered an idol. This reservation of the original meaning of idolatry will be important as we continue forward in our study, especially as we take into account the New Testament writers' pleas to avoid it. They believed that the gods were still very active during the period of the church (1 John 5:21, "Little children, keep yourselves from idols" NKJV), and so should we.

One of the questions which has likely come to mind while reading *Supernatural* and this study guide is how the term "monotheism" is supposed to work. Traditional orthodoxy requires the belief in only one God. So how are we to also believe in *other gods* if there is only one? To be clear, monotheism does not disallow belief in the gods of the first commandment, provided we clarify our terms. Notice how we apply the capital "G" to the phrase "only one God." We do this to distinguish between the creator *elohim* (God) and the created *elohim* (god/s). Biblical writers, who had no capital letters to work with, could speak of both one god or many, depending on their desired emphasis. For example, Israel's *elohim* was "above all *elohim*" (Psa 95:3), meaning that he stood apart, beyond, and distinct from all other divine beings. Having said that, however, the writer also believed that his God was a unique *elohim* among other *elohim* (Psa 96:4, "He is to be feared above all gods" NKJV). Israel's God was an *elohim*, but none of the other *elohim* compared to him. Monotheism is thus a matter of comparison, a declaration of the Creator's uniqueness and his exclusive claim upon Abraham's family in all matters of authority, power, and worship. We can be monotheists and believe that other elohim exist.

Discussion Questions

- To hear Ephesians 2:2 tell it, Satan currently has authority in our world. What physical evidence do we have that this is true? Or is this something that can only be understood by faith?

- What difference would it make to your understanding of the Bible if Jesus appeared in the Old Testament? How would it make the story different, especially in the Gospels?

- How have your heard others define idols? Why do you think that idols have become identified with cars and boats and money?

- In this discussion of cosmic geography, consider the idea of a "haunted" place. Have you ever experienced what you take be a haunted location? What does the present lordship of Jesus Christ have to say about the idea of so-called haunted places?

CHAPTER 4

KEEPING TO THE SAME STORYLINE

Read Supernatural, *chapters 7–8. Read and prepare to discuss*
Exodus 3:1–14; Leviticus 16:1–10; Deuteronomy 5:1–10; 7:1–11.

The Big Picture

The story of Abraham and his family seems to land with a thud in Egypt (Gen 50). For the reader, God's staggering promise to his faithful follower is left unrealized, and God himself appears powerless against the mighty gods of Pharaoh. So maybe Abraham was wrong in believing that his *elohim* was "the judge of all the earth" (Gen 18:25). Pharaoh did not find Moses' God to have a strong résumé (Exod 5:2, "Who is the LORD that I should obey his voice and let Israel go?"), and things only got worse when the king was presented with what his court magicians saw as a cheap magic show (Exod 7:11, "The magicians of Egypt also [turned a rod into a snake] in like manner with their enchantments"). Then the story took a turn.

We can fast-forward through the 10 plagues which specifically targeted the provisions of Egypt's gods, and stand with the redeemed Israelites on the far side of the Red Sea. *What just happened?* they must have thought. Moses' interpretation revealed the larger story: "On the day after Passover the children of Israel went out with boldness in the sight of all the Egyptians. For the Egyptians were burying all their firstborn, whom the LORD had killed among them. Also on their gods the LORD had executed judgments" (Num 33:3–4 NKJV). No wonder Moses could exclaim, "Who is like You, O LORD, among the gods? Who is like You, glorious in holiness, fearful in praises, doing wonders?" (Exod 15:11 NKJV). News of Israel's God spread into the darkest of corners. Forty years later a prostitute living in Jericho told two Israelite spies, "We have heard how the LORD dried up the water of the Red Sea for you when you came out of Egypt. As soon as we heard these things, our hearts melted. ... The LORD your *elohim*, he is *elohim* in heaven above and on earth beneath!" (Josh 2:10–11). Abraham's story was a success after all.

The Main Idea

The Old Testament plotline involved far more than what the human eye could see. *This is what happens to the person who switches loyalties from created gods to the Creator God.* Maybe we are catching a glimpse of how the story ends: *So this is how God will bring us back to the garden, back home.* But the question of the New Testament still looms ahead of us, and it's easy to be confused by what appears to be a very different story. I had a junior high gym teacher who would often blow his whistle out of desperation and make his unruly mob of kids start the game over. It is sometimes assumed that this is what the New Testament is all about—God starting over.

The goal of the New Testament is still the garden, however. We will not need to adjust our story at all. Jesus was clear that he had come to complete what God the Father had started, and he made it just as clear that his disciples were to continue to take the story forward as well. God was still making a nation out of a man who had chosen to become loyal to him, though now this kingdom would include those who were previously excluded. In Paul's words and my paraphrase: "For I am not ashamed of the good news of Christ, for it is the power of God to salvation for *not just the family of Abraham any more, but for* everyone who has faith, for the Jew first and also for the Greek" (Rom 1:16). The Gentiles will be welcomed into the family of Abraham only through fierce struggle, and both sides can be held guilty for their mutual hatred. Jews considered Gentiles to be unclean, immoral, even dead. They served gods who were harsh, unmerciful, and unable to save in time of trouble. Gentile treatment of the Jew was even worse. But word of Jesus' resurrection will change the course of history, and the course of God's kingdom, forever.

Digging Deeper

God is not looking for better behavior as much as faith, or loyalty. We owe ourselves a clarification on this matter, however, as God's expectations for his people has always included basic obedience to what he said. He was not being legalistic or picky in this expectation. Think of what it means to be a parent. We aim for faithfulness and character in our children, but we expect obedience along the way as an expression of that faithfulness. The same could be said of God and his relationship with Israel. Along with the first two commandments, which had everything to do with spiritual loyalty, came the next eight. These rules simply explained how the loyalist was to go about his business, and—here was the practical result—how life would look when refusing to worship pagan gods. As the prophet Ezekiel had warned about pagan worshipers, "These men have set up their idols in their hearts, and put before them that which causes them to stumble into iniquity" (Ezek 14:2 NKJV). Breaking commandments one and two led to breaking three through ten, and far worse. Pagans were known to execute their children in the interests of pleasing their deities, an idea that God found repugnant (Jer 7:31).

An interesting question that arises in our discussion of gods is their relative power. I have heard the question stated this way: If the gods were real, could they actually *do things*? In short, the answer is yes. The Old Testament presumes they actively demonstrated their divine power and were even responsive toward their worshipers. One fascinating story tells of the king of Moab who, when fighting against Israel, decided to sacrifice his own son as an appeal to his god for help in the battle. The next thing we hear is that "there was great indignation against Israel," presumably in response to his sacrifice (2 Kgs 3:27 NKJV). The prophets of Baal were more than willing to wager that their gods could cause fire to come down from heaven and consume a sacrifice (1 Kgs 18:24). As noted above, Egyptian magicians were said to duplicate several miracles wrought by Moses and Aaron (Exod 7:11, 22; 8:7). Turning to the New Testament in a later chapter, we will witness the temporal power of demons over humans.

Knowledge in Action

One of the most careful lessons that we can learn from our study of the gods is our God's severe response to human disloyalty with regard to worship. Our religious traditions often remind us that God hates sins—presumably all sins, of all varieties, to the same degree. But the Bible does not support this idea of viewing all human sin as equally severe. A more accurate explanation would be: While all sins displease God, the Scriptures show that the sin of idolatry (i.e., disloyalty) is *the sin* which particularly expedites God's wrath and anger. For example, it's interesting that a book like Leviticus can repeatedly speak of sins and sacrifices and repentance and forgiveness, yet completely avoid any mention of words like "wrath," "anger," or "fury" in relation to God. And this is not a mere statistical anomaly. Where we *do* hear of God's anger, we're regularly given the reason why (e.g., Deut 7:4, "For they will turn your sons away from following Me, to serve other gods; so the anger of the LORD will be aroused against you and destroy you suddenly" NKJV). What makes God angry—what makes him wrathful—is the sin of disloyalty. He is a jealous God, demanding our worship.

If you grew up going to church, you've probably wondered about the role that ritual and tradition should play in the Christian experience. A careful study of pagan religion, and the worship of gods, offers help in answering this question. Part of our confusion comes in presuming that Israel's rituals were demanded of them outside of any cultural context. But history and archaeology show that Israel was like many other nations in using temples, priests, holy articles, and even ark-like boxes in the practice of their religion. The primary temptation that Israel faced, in fact, was not the differences between their traditions and that of their foreign neighbors, but the commonalities. God warned his people to "take heed to yourself that you are not ensnared to follow" pagan practices, and that they were not to "inquire after their gods, saying, 'How do these nations serve their gods?' " (Deut 12:30 NJKV). The temptation still holds true today. The challenge is not in practicing better rituals than the other religions, but in seeing the intended meaning of the rituals you already practice. We should also remind ourselves that rituals are things we do *as loyalists*, not to necessarily become loyalists. All the rituals in Leviticus are presumed to come from the "children of Israel" (Lev 1:2), or those who willingly attributed to God his due. Our God is interested in our spiritual commitments (our *believing loyalty*) before taking notice of our performance.

Discussion Questions

- Our biblical study of the gods naturally leads to a better understanding of salvation, and God's demand of loyalty from his human creation. Why do you think God places so high a priority on faithfulness? What does this say about his character?

  _____

  _____

  _____

- Many people struggle with God's high estimation of a man like David, who was said to be a man "after God's own heart" even though he committed some notoriously bad sins. Read Psalm 23 and comment on how you see David's statements of loyalty in this poem.

  _____

  _____

  _____

- What was it about foreign gods that was seemingly so appealing to the Israelites? In other words, why did they so frequently give up worshiping the God of Abraham?

  _____

  _____

  _____

- Can you predict how our upcoming study will connect the gods of the Old Testament to the demonic forces of the New Testament—and why Jesus will perform exorcisms?

  _____

  _____

  _____

CHAPTER 5

JESUS AND THE LOVE OF GOD

Read Supernatural, *chapters 9–10. Read and prepare to discuss Numbers 13:27–33; Joshua 11:16–23; Jeremiah 7:1–19; Luke 24:13–27.*

The Big Picture

Joshua's conquest of Canaan was a military battle which carried theological meaning:

> When the LORD your God delivers them over to you, you shall conquer them and utterly destroy them. You shall make no covenant with them ... for they will turn your sons away from following Me, to serve other gods; so the anger of the LORD will be aroused against you and destroy you suddenly (Deut 7:2, 4 NKJV).

These instructions offer an eerie forecast of the future. Because Israel was not careful to destroy the Canaanites, they eventually served their gods, all too willingly.

It would take another conquest, by another Savior, to correct what had gone wrong the first time.

The names Joshua and Jesus are nearly identical in meaning ("The LORD saves"). Their ministries also carried a similar theme, connected by Nehemiah's promise: "In the time of [Israel's] trouble, when they cried to you [God] ... You gave them deliverers who saved them from the hand of their enemies" (Neh 9:27 NKJV). When the New Testament authors say that Jesus came to *save his people*, then, we cannot forget the cosmic nature of what was at stake. God's people were sinners, yes, but their sin primarily concerned their love of other gods. The first and greatest commandment had been broken; Adam's sin of obeying the voice of another deity had been repeated again and again, exciting God's wrath. This is why Jesus' arrival on the scene, like that of Joshua's, can best be explained in terms of cosmic war. Something—or someone—was about to give.

The Main Idea

The Old Testament era closed with a rhetorical question: "O LORD God of our fathers, are You not God in heaven, and do You not rule over all the kingdoms of the nations?" (2 Chr 20:6 NKJV). While we would like to answer this with an "Of course," there were no visible signs of God's authority left in Israel. As the New Testament begins, Israel had been serving other nations and their gods for over 400 years. They worshiped in a rebuilt temple, but its priests had been imported from Egypt and Mesopotamia by the wicked King Herod, and emblems of Rome's gods were openly scattered throughout its precincts. John the Baptist warned that an "axe was laid at the base of the tree" (Luke 3:9), depicting the seeming end to Israel's chance at salvation. God had had enough.

We recall Jesus' famous words given in the temple—"You have made my Father's house a den of thieves"—but we need to remember that he was quoting Jeremiah:

> Has this house, which is called by My name, become a den of thieves in your eyes? Behold I, even I, have seen it. ... The children gather wood, the fathers kindle the fire, and the women knead their dough to make cakes for the queen of heaven; and they pour out drink offerings to other gods, that they may provoke Me to anger (Jer 7:11, 18 NKJV).

The principal challenge laid down by Jesus in the temple did not concern the inappropriate selling of animals. No, this was a cosmic war that Jesus was engineering, spanning Satan's temptation in the wilderness on the front end and his death by crucifixion on the back end. Jesus' table-turning tour of the temple, while certainly famous, was just one part of this 30-year-story in the making. It was a small move in reclaiming spiritual and physical authority.

Digging Deeper

"Out of sight, out of mind." This may be how we recall a half-hearted romance that ended because of time and distance. As it turned out, this was Israel's relationship to God during their exile in Babylon (Jer 12:2, God was "far from their mind"). So what happens when we stop worshiping the right God? The Bible does not portray the human condition as ever working in a pure vacuum. We are designed to obey, whether listening to the voice of one god or another. This will be Jesus' presumption as he ministered to those who thought they were following the right god but were not. Jesus tied worship to action: "You are of your father the devil, and the desires of your father you want to do" (John 8:44 NKJV). In all of our discussion about the worship of other gods, remember that this worship always finds its expression in how a person acts. We either serve God or Mammon; there is no third option.

Much has been made in *Supernatural* and this study guide about the flow of narrative that connects one story to another in the Bible. This appreciation of the larger story lies behind the strength of keeping the reality of plural gods central to our understanding of the Bible. It certainly ties much of the Old Testament together, as we have seen. But what about the New Testament? As we turn our attention to Jesus and the ministry of the apostles, notice with vivid freshness how nicely the story continues. We shouldn't think of Jesus as a re-start to what went wrong in the Old Testament. He claims to *fulfill*—that's a positive term—what had been promised to come, especially with regard to the identity and future of the gods who had so negatively affected mankind after Genesis 3. An early sermon of Peter offers a hint of what Jesus did, and where our story is about to take us: "The word which God sent to the children of Israel, preaching peace through Jesus Christ ... who went about doing good and healing all who were oppressed by the devil ... Him God raised the third day" (Acts 10:36–40 NKJV).

Knowledge in Action

"God is Love." If there is a more common sentiment in American Christianity, we may have a hard time finding it. God's love begins almost every conversation having to do with the Gospel. Yet we all know that this concept is difficult to embrace when all the facts are known. God's words of love are often framed with words of judgment (say John 3:16 to yourself!). Our non-Christian friends may a difficult time understanding how these two ideas go together, and we should too. So let's find a helpful way to frame God's love and ... well, whatever is the opposite.

Recall the scene of Psalm 82:1: "God stands in the congregation of the mighty; He judges among the gods" (NKJV). The judgment handed down is not loving: "How long will you judge unjustly?" God asks the created spirits that have misused their power over the humans of the earth (82:2). The punishment upon these gods is stated at the end of the Psalm: "You shall perish" (82:7).

So there we have the opposite of God's love—his judgment—predicted to come upon spirit beings. This is likely what Jesus was referring to when he said that eternal punishment was designed for "the devil and his angels" (Matt 25:41). But might this judgment also refer to human punishment? Consider what came in the middle of Psalm 82: "They do not know, nor do they understand; they walk about in darkness; all the foundations of the earth are unstable" (82:5 NKJV). Is it possible that the "they" in this verse refers to the humans who follow these gods?

It appears this is precisely what God is telling these gods, and (by way of publishing this Psalm for all to hear) telling the nations as well. Those humans who love and worship created gods are wicked for doing so, and these will share in the destiny of the gods they worship. "The ungodly will not stand in the judgment" (Psa 1:5) matches Paul's later warning that those who "walk according to the prince of the power of the air, the spirit who now works in the sons of disobedience" will someday feel the "wrath" of God (Eph 2:2-3). Everyone in the end shares the destiny of the god he or she worships. This, then, would be the proper way to define the love of God, and the love of Jesus his Son. There are those who, because of their worship of the Father through the Son, experience an intimate love where "the very hairs of your head are numbered" (Matt 10:30), and yet there also will be those who in Jesus' next breath are "denied before my Father who is in heaven" because of their choice to be disloyal to the Son (Matt 10:33). Love and judgment coexist in the character and plan of God.

Discussion Questions

- Joshua's Canaanite genocide has always been difficult to match up with God's love for humanity. In times past, how have you understood Joshua's genocide?

  _____

  _____

  _____

- Why would Jesus' statement to Nicodemus that he "did not come to condemn the world" (John 3:15) be a surprise to the Jewish audience? (Hint: Think of how a Jew thought of the Gentile world, and what a messiah was promised to do to those who worshiped other gods.)

  _____

  _____

  _____

- What do you think Satan's plan for Jesus was? Did he want to see Jesus die? Why or why not? And how do you know?

  _____

  _____

  _____

- Read Colossians 2:14. What did the death of Jesus accomplish in regards to Satan's power and authority?

  _____

  _____

  _____

CHAPTER 6

BELIEVING IN JESUS' AUTHORITY

Read Supernatural, *chapters 11–12. Read and prepare to discuss Daniel 7:9–14; Luke 4:1–13; Mark 9:2–8; Matthew 26:59–66.*

The Big Picture

By noticing that the gods of the first commandment are leading characters in the story of the Bible, we soon realize that the plotline of this story may be difficult to follow. This is because a society of spirits operates primarily outside of our senses. We should also catch ourselves wondering how this grand story will end, even questioning if a happy conclusion is possible. Placing evil gods in control of the world does not bode well for the humans who live under their watch! We may wonder, "Will God ever take back the authority he gave away to the gods he created? If so, how would he do it? Will the gods give back their authority peaceably? What will God do to these gods?

And what will happen to us humans?" We certainly have a vested interest in considering how our own story ends.

In our reading from *Supernatural*, we recounted how two of the most important texts of the Bible combined to answer the question of how God would go about reclaiming his authority over the earth. The first text, the vision of Daniel 7, offers the provocative picture of a human figure approaching God's throne on a cloud in full view of his heavenly court. Then something very unexpected takes place: "To Him was given dominion and glory and a kingdom, that all peoples, nations, and languages should serve Him" (Dan 7:14 NKJV). This vision predicted that a man would someday be given control of God's creation, with the court of gods left looking on. As the vision concludes, this man further bestows this kingdom to "people, the saints of the Most High" (Dan 7:28).

The second text, another courtroom scene, takes place in Matthew 26 as Jesus was facing the Jewish high priest Caiaphas. Jesus had been silent before his accuser until being asked to respond to a direct question: "Are you the messiah, the Son of God?" The title *messiah* refers primarily to a conquerer or a king, someone who claimed victory for others in times of crisis. Jesus' answer was equally direct: "You will see the Son of Man sitting at the right hand of authority, coming on the clouds of heaven" (Matt 26:64). It was as though he opened a Bible, took hold of Caiaphas' finger, and placed it on Daniel 7:14. So now we have an idea, even if only initially, how God will reclaim his authority away from the gods of the Old Testament. He will do it through Jesus Christ.

The Main Idea

Caiaphas was so angered by Jesus' claim to authority that he sentenced him to crucifixion. Jesus therefore died because he was simply following through on a promise made to him (and the Israelite nation) in Daniel 7. The problem was clear, however: Authority would not be handed over without a fight. The Gospel writers were familiar with Old Testament teaching about the power and authority of pagan deities. This is why the public ministry of Jesus began with a confrontation with Satan and continued with exorcising demons and evil spirits from their human hosts. If your *cosmic geography* alarm is ringing at this point, you are catching why the Gospels sound as they do. Jesus came to "bear witness of the truth" of his authority (John 18:37), especially among those living in the "Galilee of the Gentiles" (Matt 4:15). Most Jews lived in southern Israel, near Jerusalem. But not Jesus. He grew up in Nazareth, a Roman military outpost, and chose Galileans—not those young rabbinical interns living near the temple—for his disciples. His travels seem to take him on repeat visits to places like Sidon and Tyre and Samaria and Caesarea Philippi, all places where foreign gods were openly worshiped and where pagan influence was abundant. None of this was accidental. He wanted to make his case for authority in front of those who needed to hear it most. The Messiah, the rightful King, would have it no other way.

Digging Deeper

A common understanding of the Old Testament in Jesus' day included the view that God would destroy the Gentiles when he came to save Israel. This was because Gentiles were presumed to worship other gods, making them the sworn enemy of official Judaism. But Gentiles were not the only enemies of God's people; this list also included the diseased (their sickness was thought to be the result of unrepentant sin), the tax collectors (an occupation which required rejection of Jewish heritage), and the prostitutes (a clear renunciation of Jewish morals). Jesus was often seen with these kinds of people, however. The reason for his compassion may have come from his reading of the important text we noted before, Psalm 82:5: "[The human followers of the gods] do not know, nor do they understand; they walk about in darkness; all the foundations of the earth are unstable" (NKJV). This may be our strongest clue in understanding what Jesus meant by coming to seek and save the lost (Luke 19:10) and not the righteous (Matt 9:13; Mark 2:17; Luke 5:32). He came to help those under the influence of evil spirit authority by introducing them to his own authority. Many Gentiles changed their loyalties to Jesus during his ministry.

We may now understand why there were no recorded demonic exorcisms in the Old Testament. If our understanding of cosmic geography is accurate, it stands
to reason that evil spirits would have felt comfortable in
the surroundings of Canaan, among the "lost" that Jesus
came to save. This was their home territory, allotted to
them by the God of Israel. So while we may hear of the periodic story where a god is silenced or shamed (Exod 8:18;
1 Kgs 18:26), we would not expect demon exorcisms as part
of the Old Testament story. Exorcisms surface in the Gospels because the truly authoritative human being from
Daniel 7 has arrived. Demons consistently describe Jesus
with uncanny accuracy: "What have we to do with You, Jesus of Nazareth? Did You come to destroy us? I know who
You are—the Holy One of God!" (Mark 1:24 NKJV). It is as
though they were aware of Daniel 7, waiting only for the
prophecy to come true.

On this account, let's draw our attention to an early
creed of the Christian faith found in 1 Timothy 3:16. Paul
introduced these six phrases as the "mystery of our religion," or what early Christians believed: "Jesus was man-
ifested in the flesh, justified in the Spirit, seen by angels,
preached among the Gentiles, believed on in the world,
and received up into glory" (NKJV). It is that odd phrase
"seen by angels" which has confused commentators for
centuries. We may wonder why this would be important
to the gospel message. But recall what we noted all the
way back in the first chapter: There are no such "things"
as angels; this is a *functional term for a god*. So let's read it

45

again, the way Paul meant to be understood (and with the help of my paraphrase): "Jesus came in the flesh, and was vindicated by the Holy Spirit at his baptism; he confronted the gods of the Old Testament, and in so doing showed his authority to Gentile worshipers; many Gentiles became loyal to him, and he became Lord of all through his death and resurrection." This is the condensed *mystery of our story*, revealed through Jesus Christ.

Knowledge in Action

Have you ever wondered what would have led you to believe in Jesus if he had come through your town? For me, exorcisms would have been the most powerful influence of all. Picture the scene: I and my fellow villagers go about our days being told that the God of Israel is real but *believing that pagan gods are even more real* since we can see what they do. No human can control them, as hard as they may try. At times these gods literally take over human bodies, even causing them to injure themselves. Yet every Sabbath I hear that my God is the creator and controller of all there is. On my walk home I realize how strong my faith needs to be while I am honestly battling the temptation to give my loyalties to the powers that are all around me.

Then I hear of Jesus—and let's place ourselves into an actual story recorded in Luke 4: He steps into my synagogue (4:16), preaches a sermon from Isaiah about ministering to the needs of Gentiles (4:18-27), and survives a following assassination attempt (4:28-30). I wonder if this will deter him or cause him to reconsider his message. In following him to another synagogue, however, I hear him speak about his authority even more boldly (4:31-32). At this point, a man who is controlled by a demon (we all presumed him to be a regular worshiper!) steps forward (4:33). I hear the demon tell the crowd that he knows who Jesus is, though he is unsure what this means for his own future (4:34). Jesus quiets the god and tells him to leave the man alone (4:35). *The god obeys,* and everyone in the room is amazed (4:36-37). No one has ever seen a human tell a god what to do.

However, I would have soon realized that following Jesus took repeated steps of faith and loyalty. He did not always do what I would have expected him to do, especially if I had wanted him to be a strong Jewish leader who would rid the nation of Gentile influence. He instead befriended the very Gentiles I did not like and scolded the Jewish leaders I respected. At one point he told his followers that he had a "new commandment ... to love one another" (John 13:34), as though he could speak directly for the God of Israel. The hardest step of faith, of course, was following Jesus to the point of his own death, knowing that his exorcisms had already proved his authority over every human or divine power. I needed to believe that he died on purpose, and for a purpose.

Discussion Questions

- Do you think Jesus' exorcisms would have had a powerful affect upon you? How would you have interpreted them?

  _____

  _____

  _____

- At this point in our study, are you able to define the gospel in terms of authority, and how Jesus had come to fulfill the vision of Daniel 7?

  _____

  _____

  _____

- Are you able to feel the kind of hatred and disgust that Jews had for Gentiles in the days of Jesus? Why is this an important emotion to identify with in understanding the story of the Bible?

  _____

  _____

  _____

- Looking ahead in the story, why do you think God chose to ultimately defeat evil spirits and Satan by having Jesus die?

_____

_____

_____

CHAPTER 7

THE CHURCH AS GOD'S PRESENCE

Read Supernatural, *chapters 13–14. Read and prepare to discuss* *Acts 2:1–8; 16:11–34; Ephesians 1:15–23; 1 Peter 3:14–22.*

The Big Picture

You can't run from God is a good lesson we can learn from the book of Jonah. The book's critical lesson, however, and the one that Jonah struggled to understand while watching Nineveh avoid divine punishment, is that *God loves Gentiles too.* Jews struggled mightily to understand that their God's grace was big enough for the entire world. This is why the stories of Rahab, Ruth, and the people of Nineveh were so important in the Old Testament, and why Peter and Paul viewed their ministries as so important in the New Testament. The "good news" is that Jesus Christ has become Lord of both heaven and earth through his death and resurrection, and thereby the Lord of the Gentile nations as well. Continuing to serve other gods would not only be senseless, but wicked. Jesus was coming back to judge the world for its disloyalty to God.

The summons of the gospel, or the action it requires us to take, involves one simple word: faith. We need to believe that Jesus Christ is Lord, and that every god now submits to him. This is what Jesus meant when he said "All authority is now given to me in heaven and on earth" as he was about to ascend (Matt 28:18). The disciples had learned of this authority over the past three years, watching numerous demonic exorcisms. But they were not expecting his next words: "Go and make disciples of all the nations" (28:19). As Jewish disciples of a Jewish messiah, they were prepared to hear, "make disciples of your Jewish countrymen." *But it was the Gentiles they were to go after, just like Jonah*, they realized. In short, the disciples would have interpreted Jesus as declaring a kind of cosmic war. They were commanded by their messiah to invade Gentile cities (the world was 93 percent Gentile at this time) and proclaim the news, the "gospel," that Jesus was Lord. And this meant that Caesar was not.

The Main Idea

The church was intended to become God's new physical presence in the world. What we mean by *physical presence* needs clarification, however. Most people think that a church is a building on a corner, something designed and built for large groups of people to meet and worship in. But this was not what *church* meant in the New Testament.

"Church" referred to people—*believers*. Listen to one of the first letters that the Apostle Paul wrote to a Christian group, in this case in Thessalonica:

> Your faith has gone out, so that we do not need to say anything. For they themselves [other believers in the area] declare ... how you turned to God from idols to serve the living and true God, and to wait for his Son from heaven whom he raised from the dead, even Jesus who delivers us from the wrath to come (1 Thess 1:8–10 NKJV adapted).

Imagining what Paul might have meant by the *physical presence* of God in a local city, picture this scene: A man and his wife set out from their home to meet with others who have come to believe that Jesus Christ is the true Son of God and Lord of the world. The coins in their pocket said that Caesar Augustus was "The Son of God," but they knew this wasn't true. They walk past a statue of the city deity and do not bow. They are invited to join a festival dedicated to the god of a rich man's estate and turn away. They carry with them no idols or religious trinkets. When they buy a loaf of bread the merchant asks which god they will be praying to that evening. "Jesus," they say. "And since you asked, he is the Nazarene who died, was buried, and who was raised by God in order to prove that he is the King of the world and the guarantee of our own resurrection in the future."

Establishing this kind of physical presence in every town was God's intention for a missionary such as Paul.

This church would not be judged by size or by wealth, but by cosmic power displayed in Jesus-directed loyalty. God predicted how the church would look when he commissioned Paul to spread the gospel: "[I am sending you] to open [the Gentiles'] eyes, and turn them from darkness to light, and from the power of Satan to God" (Acts 26:18 NKJV). Whenever this happened, wherever this happened, the physical presence of God was made very, very real.

Digging Deeper

Taking the news of Jesus' lordship into the Gentile world certainly drew a strong reaction. Resistance was everywhere, coming from all directions. Nonbelieving Gentiles certainly didn't like hearing that a crucified Jew had ascended to a position of lordship over their own gods (this sometimes resulted in stoning; e.g., Acts 14:19). Many pagans did not believe in the idea of physical resurrection (see Acts 17:32) and therefore rejected the apostles' message outright. Even Jews who accepted Jesus struggled in sharing his lordship with Gentiles. This was because all non-Jews were considered ritually unclean and thus unable to approach the God of Israel unless they converted to Judaism (Acts 10:13–15). In combining all these forces, we can see why Paul said that the gospel was a "stumbling block to the Jews and foolishness to the Greeks" (1 Cor 1:23).

So why were missionaries such as Paul persecuted? Modern Christianity has a difficult time imagining what caused this phenomenon in the New Testament era, as we are used to a live-and-let-live religious climate. Once again we need to read the Bible as it was meant to be read, believing with its original audience that the gods were very real and very active. Imagine for a moment that someone came into town teaching that your pagan deity, the god that your ancestors prayed to for generations, was now bowing in reverence to a crucified and resurrected Nazarene you had never heard of. This was no small matter. Changing your worship patterns meant tempting your fate. Your wife may become barren if you worshiped the wrong god, or even the right god in the wrong way. To convert to Christianity was tantamount to upsetting the natural and spiritual order of everything you knew and depended upon. It would be safer, thus better, to beat and even torture the person who suggested worshiping another god.

With the above in mind, we should also take a moment to understand why baptism was so important to the first-century world, and why this ritual was so important to the pagan world of gods and deities. While we often think of baptism as a biblical tradition, we are not sure when and where the physical display of dunking in water originated. It seems to have started after Malachi and before Matthew. One thing is for sure, however: When a person was baptized in the ancient world, they were advertising to the watching world their spiritual loyalties, and all that went along with this. Lydia, for example, was baptized immediately after (as the text so beautifully says) God had opened her heart to believe what Paul was telling her about Jesus (Acts 16:14–15). She seems to have been a Gentile who worshiped the God of Israel before coming to believe in Jesus. Baptized just hours later was the Philippian jailer, who placed his loyalties in the "Lord Jesus Messiah" (Acts 16:31) that very evening. What's important to visualize is what is implied but not explicitly stated: As Lydia and the jailer resumed their daily lives after baptism, they were now "outed" in their communities as Christ-followers. They could no longer hide behind their faith in Jesus, and persecution may have followed. Baptism seems to have been the most powerful conversion statement in the early church, and we can only imagine the hostilities it caused in this idol-crazed pagan world.

Knowledge in Action

Let's pause and ask our leading question once again: Are the gods of the Old Testament real spiritual beings? Yes, we have argued, the evidence of Scripture leads us to this conclusion. It is only when the gods are real that the first commandment retains its original meaning. The problem of spiritual disloyalty also becomes very dangerous, just as the Bible describes. God's jealousy can be very real, even proper or expected. The demons that met Jesus can be real and powerful. The punishment promised to the world for following after these gods can be real as well. And, as we have noticed above, the ministry of the apostles in the book of Acts can be meaningful. A few more practical thoughts on this idea are warranted.

The final commission of Jesus in Matthew 28 bears remarkable solidarity to the story that begins in Genesis. This is because Jesus came to solve the problem which the Old Testament had so carefully set out to describe: "Now I say that Jesus Christ has become a servant to the circumcision [Jews] for the truth of God, to confirm the promises made to the fathers, and that the Gentiles might glorify God for His mercy" (Rom 15:8–9 NKJV). There we have it—as succinct an explanation of why Jesus came to earth as we may ever read in the Bible: He came to keep a promise for one group of people, and to surprise another group of people. The promise kept was for the Jew, who had been chosen by God but had become a nation of idolaters. The surprise was for the Gentiles, who had been delegated to live under the authority of evil spiritual powers. In defeating these powers, whether during his ministry or at the crucifixion, Jesus demonstrated mercy to the Gentiles.

The opening commission of the apostles in Acts 2 also bears remarkable similarity to the situation described in Genesis 11. As *Supernatural* noted, God's allotment of physical territory to evil gods in Genesis 11 (as rehearsed in Deut 32 and elsewhere) led to the migration of the problem of god-worship over the entire world. So it is fitting that the solution to the problem migrates as well. "Everyone heard the disciples speak in their own language ... we hear them telling the wonderful works of God" (Acts 2:6, 11). The comparison is hard to ignore: The common language spoken by the people at Babel (Gen 11:1) helped them unite against God and build a structure designed to worship other gods. The distinct languages of Acts 2:4 reverses this original "babel" (a Hebrew term that means confusion). In this way, the Spirit empowered Jews at Pentecost to hear about Jesus, believe the gospel, and then go back to their distant homes. Pagans would now hear about Jesus.

In trying to understand the relationship of Genesis 11 and Acts 2, some have wondered if a "map" of demonic strongholds is able to be found in the biblical narrative. *Supernatural* details some possibilities that seem to surface in the Old Testament, and it is possible that some stories hint to a cosmic geography that is beyond our knowledge (some commentators have wondered, for example, if Jacob crossed a divine boundary of some kind when crossing the Jabbok River and meeting the angel who fought him; see Gen 32:22–24). Whatever the case, the New Testament seems to purposely quell our curiosities about demonic strongholds by withholding any kind of map of demonic activity. Indeed, Paul seems to broaden Satan's territorial influence by calling him "the prince and power of the air" (Eph 2:2), and the writer of 1 John seems to agree that we should see Satan's power as worldwide, not subjected to political or natural boundaries (1 John 5:19, "the whole world lays under the authority of the wicked one").

Discussion Questions

- We have made much of the biblical story of God including the Gentile into the family of Abraham through Jesus Christ. How might this story apply to you? In other words, who is the Gentile in your own life, and what are you to do about it?

  _____

  _____

  _____

- God wants his presence "felt" in our world, even though he is spirit. How can your faith in Jesus' lordship over the gods of the world become something that is visible, even physical?

  _____

  _____

  _____

- From what you are learning, and from what you know about Paul's personality, why do you think Paul enjoyed going where "Christ had not been previously named" (Rom 15:20)?

  _____

  _____

  _____

- When we consider what God wants the church to be in any given community, why might five small churches be better than one large one?

_____

_____

_____

CHAPTER 8

BECOMING DIVINE

Read Supernatural, *chapters 15–16. Read and prepare to discuss Galatians 3:26–29; Ephesians 1:3–6; Romans 8:15–23; 2 Peter 2:1–4; Revelation 3:19–22; 22:1–5.*

The Big Picture

"For all have sinned, and fall short of the glory of God" (Rom 3:23). This verse is well-known, but still full of mystery. The verb translated as "fall short" appears in the present tense, meaning that we currently lack the glory of God. The next question to ask is "What do we mean by glory?" A hint appears ahead in Romans 8:18: "For I consider the sufferings of the present time are not worthy to be compared to the glory which will be revealed in us" (NKJV adapted). Then Paul drops the bombshell: "For the creation eagerly waits for the revelation of the sons of God" (8:19). In putting all these pieces together, we realize that Paul believes that the *glory of God* is someday coming to the Christian, and that it will include the idea of becoming *sons of God.*

This is a heavy truth, and *Supernatural* properly waits until its final pages to explain what it means. Christian theologians have described this as the *divinization* of mankind, appealing to the promise of 2 Peter 1:4: "That through these [great and precious promises] you may be partakers of the divine nature [*theios*], having escaped the corruption that is in the world through lust" (NKJV). The word we itch to understand is *theios*, which is the adjective equivalent of the noun *theos* ("God/god"), recommending to us the odd but accurate idea of "god-ish." The promise is mind-boggling, but it's right there in the text. The believer will someday become *god-ish* or *god-like* (see 1 John 3:1–3). It is a promise we cannot begin to understand, but one which compels us to appreciate what we have learned about the gods that rule our present world.

The Main Idea

What is the final goal in our Christian journey? Traditionally, we have assumed that going to heaven is our great and final hope, leaving this earth and body behind to enjoy bliss in a spiritual existence quite unlike our own. The biblical promise, however, begins and ends quite differently. Our goal starts by following Jesus' pattern in receiving a resurrected body: "Now Christ is risen from the dead, and has become the firstfruits [first among others] of those who have died" (1 Cor 15:20 NKJV adapted). This is what it means, ultimately, to be "in Christ," or identified with the messiah (15:22). We receive what he received—a resurrected body.

But the goal of our afterlife does not end with the resurrection. Paul makes a curious connection *backward* in Galatians 3:29: "If you are Christ's, then you are Abraham's seed" (NKJV). It is as though Paul is saying *the story becomes complete only when we revisit the beginning to become what we were originally intended to be.* The original intention, we recall, was that the family of Abraham would bless the world through its covenant with God. Abraham was chosen to be blessed, but not for his sake alone. It appears that Paul's Christ-to-Abraham connection places the resurrected believer back into the *position of being a blessing* as Abraham was. We are identified not only with Christ, but with Abraham. We fulfill both of their stories.

But this only leads us to ask, "Who will the resurrected believer bless in the next world?" Here we must tread rather lightly, as there is much we do not know. Listening to the Bible describe our afterlife is like reading signposts pointing into a fog, as one writer says. But Paul adds an important piece to the puzzle when he makes the comment, still in Galatians 3:29, that when we are in Abraham we are actually "heirs according to the promise." So we are heirs ... of what? We are pushed back once again to the start of the story—back to Eden.

We all have sinned and fall short, presently, of the glory of God. Let's use the idea of *stewardship* for *glory* here, as we talked about before (Prov 25:2, "It is the glory of kings to search out a matter"), and adjust our vision of the future by looking backward one last time: Our sin has resulted in our present failure to "have the glory of God," or be God's proper stewards over creation. We were kicked out of the garden, and this stewardship was given to someone else—who ended up abusing it terribly. Turning this around, the day is coming when we will become God's stewards once again, "heirs of God and joint heirs with Christ ... glorified together" (Rom 8:17 NKJV). This seems to be the fulfillment of our "inheritance." In some sense we will be doing what Christ is doing, ruling with him over a global Eden (Rev 3:21; 21:1-4; 22:1-5), even ruling over the spirit world (1 Cor 6:3). This is apparently what it means, in part, to be *theios*, or god-ish.

Digging Deeper

Hearing about a doctrine for the first time can be unsettling. The concept of *theosis*, or becoming "partakers of the divine nature" (2 Pet 1:4 NKJV), is an example of a biblical teaching that often surprises people who have attended church all their lives. The fact is, this teaching appears in some denominational traditions but not in others. Don't let that alarm you. If you are a part of the Western church tradition, which includes the Roman Catholic Church and the Protestant denominations which originated in the 16th century, you likely have not been taught about the doctrine of *theosis* (even though the refomers discussed it in their writings). In its place the emphasis has been the doctrine of justification, defined as that moment when

God graciously declared you to be righteous because of Christ's work on your behalf. If your background is the Eastern church tradition (Greek Orthodox, Russian Orthodox, etc.), *theosis* has been a regular part of your liturgy and catechetical training. Your understanding of justification differs from the Western tradition because it is combined with the doctrine of *theosis*. In this view, God both *considers* the believing person righteous and actually *accomplishes* righteousness in that person by making him god-like.

Now may also be a good time, as we are nearing the conclusion of our study, to consider why the general topic of this book may have seemed to be new for you. Many people who hear about the idea of a divine council of gods respond with something like "Why haven't I heard of this before?" or even "How can this be true if I have never heard of it before?" We grant that the idea of other gods ruling in the heavens by God's design is not commonly taught in the church. I personally came to believe this view about a dozen years ago, as I was in the final days of finishing my doctoral degree at an evangelical seminary. I decided to write my dissertation on the Old Testament concept of plural deities as the backdrop of the principalities and powers of Paul's letters. After studying the topic, I became more convinced than ever that this was how the Bible was intended to be read and understood.

In my experience there are several reasons why this view is still rather unknown. First, while many scholarly books and articles have been written about the topic of gods, spirits, and angels over the years, most of the authors are not trying to communicate to the popular evangelical audience. We are simply not reading their material. Second, the subject of angels and gods has been subjected to an inordinate amount of tradition as compared to other Christian doctrines. We are more influenced by Hollywood than the Bible when considering who angels are and what they do (for example, imagine for a moment what Satan looks like!). The third reason for not hearing about this topic is possibly the most unfortunate of all. In my opinion, the passages that talk so plainly about the gods of the Old Testament have simply not been allowed to speak for themselves. The most clear or plain reading of the text has become lost. It is my hope that through this study you may once again read the Bible the way it was meant to be understood.

Knowledge in Action

Reading the Bible as it was meant to be understood. So easy to say, not so easy to do! We are all trying to read the Bible properly, and we believe this starts by trying to understand what the biblical authors meant to convey to their original audience. We have also spoken often of understanding the story of the Bible, or seeing where its broad narrative was headed. The original writers of Scripture were vitally interested in keeping the gods (their character, their activity, their danger, their future, etc.) near the center of everything the Bible was trying to describe.

They form, to a large degree, the very *worldview* of the Bible. C. S. Lewis is remembered for his famous explanation of what it means to have a worldview: "I believe in Christianity as I believe that the sun has risen. Not only because I see it, but because by it I see everything else." Some elements of a story are so important that they help everything else in the story come into focus.

Our understanding of *theosis* is meant to adjust our hope for our futures, but even more important, influence our present lives as followers of Christ. Can any of us really understand what it means to become *god-like*? Not yet. But we can understand how "We brought nothing into this world, and it is certain that we can carry nothing out" (1 Tim 6:7 NKJV). Paul was no less excited to talk about our present Christian journey—the all-too-familiar path of suffering that has been gifted to us by Jesus—than he was to speak of our future home on a re-created earth with resurrected bodies. Our Savior invited us to partake in his present kingdom by living out our time in "loving one another—as I have loved you, love also one another" (John 13:34). *Theosis* can wait.

What shall we make of our present situation, then, as we await the ultimate rule of Christ over the gods of the Old Testament and "rulers and authorities" of the New Testament? Paul describes the conclusion of the story:

> Then comes the end, when [Jesus] delivers the kingdom to God the Father, when He puts an end to all [of the gods' present] rule and all authority and

power. For He must reign till He has put all enemies under His feet. The last enemy that will be destroyed is death. ... Now when all things are made subject to [Jesus], then the Son Himself will also be subject to Him who put all things under Him, that God may be all in all (1 Cor 15:24–26, 28 NKJV).

The victory trumpet has blown, but our battle continues as though we are fighting through a fog, waiting for the mist to lift so we can see our Leader in his full glory.

Discussion Questions

- What does the fact of resurrection teach you about the importance of your present physical body?

  _____

  _____

  _____

- How does the doctrine of *theosis* adjust how you understand your afterlife?

  _____

  _____

  _____

- In your opinion, what was God's larger purpose in creating the gods, and giving them the authority they now have?

  _____

  _____

  _____

- How will your present outlook on life change because of this study?

  _____

  _____

  _____

KNOWING WHERE TO TINKER

My opening story of Charles Steinmetz tinkering with Henry Ford's assembly line was meant to illustrate the main challenge of this book and *Supernatural*: not to read a different Bible, but to read the Bible differently—tinkering with one small element of the process on the front end and noticing what a large difference it can make by the time you are done. It is easy to read the same Bible over and over, getting the same result over and over, unless we make a conscious effort to change *how* we read the Bible. I like to compare Bible interpretation with test-driving a car, where experimentation is a good thing. I can take the Bible "out for a drive" using one interpretation, then take it out again following a different interpretation. I see which ride goes more smoothly, or which one allows the car's engine to run to its full potential. I have found this to be a fun and time-consuming way to read the Bible, but very profitable as well.

Because of the amount of material covered in *Supernatural* and this study guide, it may be helpful to rewind and recall some of those moments that have "tinkered" with your understanding of the Bible. I will limit our review to five main points.

First, remember that the beings called *gods* in the Bible are to be understood as real, personal beings who exist in a realm we cannot see or feel. We should vigorously avoid the common temptation to think of these gods as imaginary or "false." Sometimes the Bible will refer to these beings as *spirits* or *angels* or even *demons*, and we need to keep in mind that these English titles are not meant to diminish the influential role these gods play in the story of Scripture.

Second, and just as foundational as our first point, it's important to remember that our Creator gave at least some of the gods a role of unprecedented authority in our human experience. We sometimes speak of God's "council" of divine beings in this sense. Whether presiding over an earthly kingdom or through less defined means, these gods enact their will upon earthly subjects. Their desire to receive worship from human beings has inflamed the jealousy and wrath of God, which is why they will someday be punished or destroyed for what they have done to our world and its population.

Third, recall that the coming of Jesus is best interpreted in terms of a cosmic war which pitted God's Son against the temporal rulers of our world. When demons met Jesus, for example, they threw themselves down in worship while many humans looked on with confusion. Demons knew who Jesus was, even pleading that he not hurt them as promised in the Old Testament. So our Messiah came to "seek and save the lost," and he did this by defeating the powers that claimed authority over these humans.

Fourth, we saw that the mission of the early church reflected the apostles' desire to take the news of Jesus' authority into all the world. The Apostle Paul wrote letters and visited churches encouraging believers to practically apply Jesus' lordship into daily experience. And even though Paul knew that Jesus was the final victor over all heavenly powers, he also believed that the Christian needed to wear a kind of "spiritual armor" in going to war against these gods at the present time (Eph 6:12).

The last main theme could be summarized by Paul's grand pronouncement in 1 Corinthians 15:24: "Then comes the end, when Jesus delivers the kingdom to God the Father, when he puts an end to all rule and authority and power." This end, of course, becomes a new beginning for the Christian. We will be resurrected with a new body and given what Peter calls a "divine nature" (2 Pet 1:4). Our life will resemble what Adam and Eve enjoyed in the garden of Eden before the fall. We will even enjoy some kind of rule and authority in the final state, even presiding over angels/gods themselves (1 Cor 6:3). So there is clearly more to "going to heaven" than simply going to heaven!

Your study of the Bible is only just beginning. Thank you for taking part in this journey. May God be glorified through your walk with Jesus Christ.

NOTES

_____

_____

_____

_____

_____

_____

_____

_____

_____

_____

_____

_____

_____

_____

_____

_____

_____

_____

_____

_____

_____

_____

_____

_____

_____

_____

_____

_____

_____

_____

_____

_____

_____

_____

_____

_____

_____

_____

_____

_____

_____

_____

_____

_____

_____

_____

_____

_____

_____

_____